My Journey Aboard

THE MAYFLOWER

By Max Caswell

Gareth Stevens
PUBLISHING

Please visit our website, www.garethstevens.com. For a free color catalog of all our high-quality books, call toll free 1-800-542-2595 or fax 1-877-542-2596.

Library of Congress Cataloging-in-Publication Data

Names: Caswell, Max, author.
Title: My journey aboard the Mayflower / Max Caswell.
Description: New York : Gareth Stevens Publishing, [2018] | Series: My place in history | Includes index.
Identifiers: LCCN 2017007148| ISBN 9781538202173 (pbk. book) | ISBN 9781538202180 (6 pack) | ISBN 9781538202197 (library bound book)
Subjects: LCSH: Mayflower (Ship)–Juvenile literature. | Pilgrims (New Plymouth Colony)–Juvenile literature.
Classification: LCC F68 .C35 2018 | DDC 973.2–dc23
LC record available at https://lccn.loc.gov/2017007148

Published in 2018 by
Gareth Stevens Publishing
111 East 14th Street, Suite 349
New York, NY 10003

Copyright © 2018 Gareth Stevens Publishing

Designer: Bethany Perl
Editor: Joan Stoltman

Photo credits: Cover, p. 1 (ship) Three Lions/Hulton Archive/Getty Images; cover, p. 1 (background) Natalia Sheinkin/Shutterstock.com; cover, pp. 1–24 (torn strip) barbaliss/Shutterstock.com; cover, pp. 1–24 (photo frame) Davor Ratkovic/Shutterstock.com; cover, pp. 1–24 (white paper) HABRDA/Shutterstock.com; cover, pp. 1–24 (parchment) M. Unal Ozmen/Shutterstock.com; cover, pp. 1–24 (textured edge) saki80/Shutterstock.com; pp. 1–24 (paper background) Kostenko Maxim/Shutterstock.com; p. 5 (landscape) DEA/A. DAGLI ORTI/De Agostini/Getty Images; p. 5 (printing office) Print Collector/Hulton Archive/Getty Images; p. 7 (Puritans) Time Life & Pictures/The LIFE Picture Collection/Getty Images; p. 7 (James I) John Decritz the Elder/Getty Images; p. 9 courtesy of Internet Archive Book Images; p. 11 (bowls of food) John Nordell/The Christian Science Monitor via Getty Images/Getty Images; p. 11 (hard tack) D. Farr/Wikipedia.org; p. 13 DEA PICTURE LIBRARY/De Agostini Picture Library/Getty Images; p. 15 Christophel Fine Art/Universal Images Group/Getty Images; p. 17 boreala/Shutterstock.com; p. 19 Jean Leon Gerome Ferris/Wikipedia.org; p. 21 Interim Archives/Archive Photos/Getty Images.

Printed in the United States of America

CPSIA compliance information: Batch #CS17GS: For further information contact Gareth Stevens, New York, New York at 1-800-542-2595.

CONTENTS

Words in the glossary appear in **bold** type the first time they are used in the text.

Heading to the
NEW WORLD

July 6, 1620, Leiden, Netherlands

Father gave me this journal to record our journey to America. He says it's important that future people know how our colony began. I promise to write at least once a month.

I'm nervous about this journey. I've never been on a ship. Father said only men have been to America, and many families are leaving their daughters in the Netherlands. America sounds dangerous and tough and scary. Thankfully, my dearest friend Abigail's family is coming, too!

Notes from History

The Separatists were a **religious** group that escaped to the Netherlands from England in the early 1600s. The Netherlands let them practice their faith, but paid them little to work long, hard hours.

In the Netherlands, their parents didn't make enough money, so even young Separatist children had to work!

Fellow TRAVELERS

July 20, 1620, Leiden, Netherlands

I was born here, but my parents and brother, Robert, were born in England. Robert told me about life in England. He said Father once went to jail because of what we believe. He said many people in England make fun of our religion.

Today, Father said some other English families will be joining us on our journey, too. They aren't part of our faith, but these "strangers" are hoping for a better life, just like us. I hope they're nice!

Notes from History

The Separatists called themselves the "saints." They called the other travelers the "strangers."

In England, the king was in charge
of the government and the church.
This meant that all other faiths were
against the law!

Finally ON THE SHIP

August 6, 1620, Dartmouth, England

I'm writing aboard the *Speedwell*, the ship our church bought in the Netherlands. We've just left Southampton, England, where we met up with the strangers and our other ship, the *Mayflower*.

Alas, it seems our dear *Speedwell* needs mending, and it might take a month to fix! We're to stay inside the ship while it's being fixed. Mother says we're already running low on food! Thank goodness Abigail and I can play with our **poppets** while we wait.

Notes from History

Years later, it was discovered the *Speedwell*'s problems happened on purpose. The Netherlands wanted the land in America the **Pilgrims** had paid to colonize, so it paid the crew to **damage** the *Speedwell*.

The *Speedwell* was half the size of the *Mayflower*, but it was considered large enough to make it across the Atlantic Ocean. The *Speedwell* was going to become the colony's fishing ship in the New World.

Leaving the
SPEEDWELL BEHIND

September 2, 1620, Plymouth, England

We set sail yesterday, but were forced to land again because of the *Speedwell*. This morning, we deserted the ship and moved onto the *Mayflower*. Food is really low!

Abigail's family didn't come with us. Her family is returning to the Netherlands. Ten other families from our church are too, because there isn't enough room aboard the *Mayflower*. Will I ever see Abigail again? Can we build our colony with so few people?

Notes from History

The journey from England to America typically took 1 month. No one knows what the Pilgrims packed, but it was probably enough food for a few months. No one knew it would take over a month just to leave England!

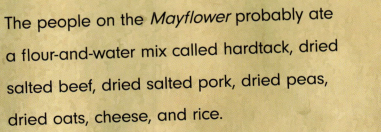

HARDTACK

The people on the *Mayflower* probably ate a flour-and-water mix called hardtack, dried salted beef, dried salted pork, dried peas, dried oats, cheese, and rice.

Life on the OPEN SEA

September 7, 1620, Atlantic Ocean

We've finally left England. I can't wait to get to America and get off this ship! This is a terrible way to live!

We're living on the gun deck. Maybe **cannons** don't mind this life, but I do! Cold seawater drips from everywhere. It's dark as midnight. The air's thick with horrible smells from the chickens and pigs, and **chamber pots** spill whenever the ship **pitches**. Father built privacy walls, but now I feel like I'm locked in a chest.

Notes from History
The *Mayflower* was built to move **cargo**. The passengers lived on the gun deck, which was usually filled with cannons to protect the cargo from pirates.

THE *MAYFLOWER*

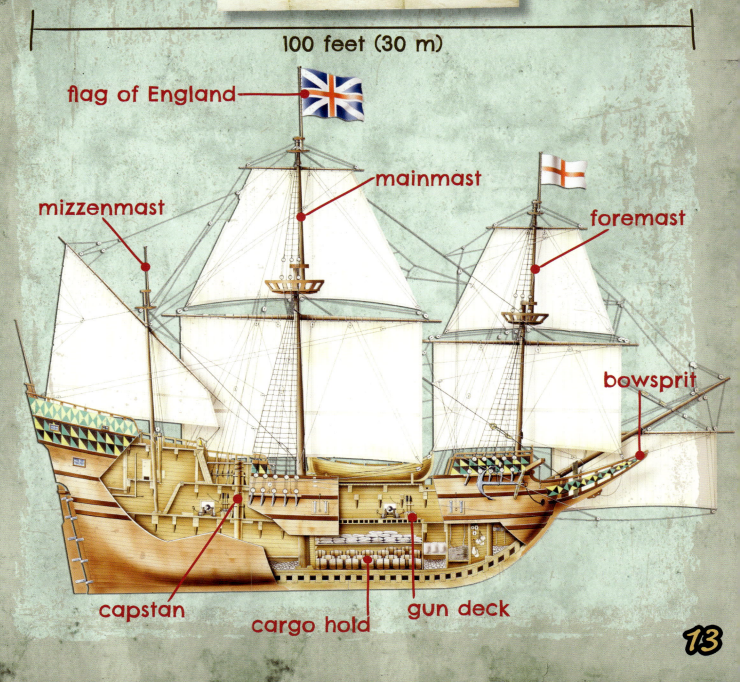

100 feet (30 m)

flag of England

mainmast

mizzenmast

foremast

bowsprit

capstan

cargo hold

gun deck

13

A Terrible STORM

October 12, 1620

Almost everyone's seasick. Yesterday's storm was so terrible, the crew made the ship lie **ahull**. The ship suddenly got very quiet. One of the saints' servants, John Howland, thought the storm had passed, so he climbed up to the main deck.

I felt the ship suddenly move just after he'd climbed up. He says he was thrown overboard! Luckily, he grabbed a rope before he fell into the ocean. The crew pulled him back onto the ship!

Notes from History

John Howland **inherited** a large amount of money and land when his master died in America. He went on to have 10 children, 88 grandchildren, and was one of the most successful of all the *Mayflower* colonists!

Many ships in the 1600s were harmed by storms, especially during the Atlantic Ocean storm season (October and November). The *Mayflower*'s height made it so hard to sail, the journey across the ocean took a month longer than it was supposed to.

NEW LIFE

November 1, 1620

Last week, Mrs. Hopkins gave birth to a boy, Oceanus. It must have been hard to give birth during a storm! Mother says Mrs. Hopkins is a strong woman.

The very next day, Master Jones saw land! Sadly, we were many miles north of the land we purchased and without a map of America's coast. After 2 days heading south, we hit terrible, rocky water. Master Jones said it was too dangerous to go any further.

Notes from History

The rocky water that would become known as Pollack Rip wasn't the only reason to turn around. The ship was filled with illness, and Master Jones needed to keep his crew healthy for the trip home!

THE *MAYFLOWER* IN THE NEW WORLD

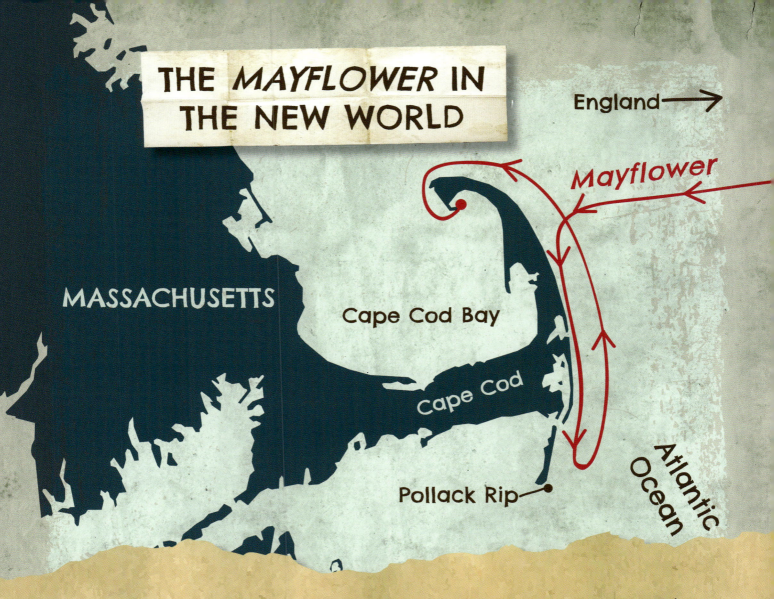

England →

Mayflower

MASSACHUSETTS

Cape Cod Bay

Cape Cod

Pollack Rip

Atlantic Ocean

The travelers lived aboard the *Mayflower* for almost a year! They spent 2 months aboard in England, 2 months at sea, and 6 more months waiting to come ashore in modern-day Massachusetts.

An AGREEMENT

November 11, 1620

Last night, the strangers announced they'd leave us once we go ashore. Father said our colony might be doomed! After I went to sleep, a paper was written for saints and strangers alike to agree to work together. Early this morning, the men signed it.

This afternoon, I saw the sun. Our new home is so quiet and hilly. Twelve men went ashore to gather wood. The warmth of a fire felt so good. America looks nothing like I imagined.

Notes from History

The paper signed aboard the *Mayflower* while in Cape Cod Bay, called the Mayflower Compact, created a government where everyone would work together for the good of the colony.

The Mayflower Compact was signed by 41 men, saints and strangers alike, including servants, but not women.

Our New HOME

February 1, 1621

It took over a month to find a place for the colony. The men found a deserted native community with freshwater and cleared fields for farming. We moved the ship closer to this spot in late December. Each day, the men drag boats filled with building supplies to the shore. Father says the water feels like ice!

Many have died from this cold wetness, but Robert, Mother, Father, and I have been lucky. Father says the houses will be ready next month!

Notes from History

The colonists spent their first winter in America aboard the *Mayflower*. Over half of the group died that winter, from overwork, **pneumonia**, and illnesses caused by not eating well.

Life in those first few months in America was filled with sickness and death, but also hope, discovery, and wonder!

GLOSSARY

ahull: with sails taken down so that a ship isn't affected by wind during a storm

cannon: a large gun that shoots heavy metal or stone balls

cargo: goods carried by a plane, train, truck, or ship

chamber pot: a pot that is kept in a bedroom and used as a toilet

damage: harm

inherit: to get by legal right after a person's death

Pilgrim: one of the first settlers in what became the United States

pitch: to have the front of a ship dive down and rise suddenly in large waves

pneumonia: a serious illness that affects the lungs and makes it hard to breathe

poppet: a doll made of cloth

religious: having to do with a belief in and way of honoring a god or gods

For more INFORMATION

Books

Cook, Peter. *You Wouldn't Want to Sail on the Mayflower! A Trip That Took Entirely Too Long.* New York, NY: Franklin Watts, 2014.

Lynch, P. J. *The Boy Who Fell off the Mayflower, or, John Howland's Good Fortune.* Somerville, MA: Candlewick Press, 2015.

Smith, Andrea P. *The Journey of the Mayflower.* New York, NY: PowerKids Press, 2012.

Websites

Mayflower II
plimoth.org/what-see-do/mayflower-ii
Read about this ship that was built to look and feel exactly like the original *Mayflower*.

Mayflower Voyage
landofthebrave.info/mayflower-passengers.htm
Read 40 fun facts about the *Mayflower* voyage!

INDEX